The Pullen's Story
1879 – Present Day

by Roger Batchelor

R. Batchelor

03/12/2017

All profits from the sale of this book will go towards building a new boys home at New Life Africa International in Nakuru, Kenya.

Revised 2014

2nd Reprint

Every effort has been made to identify and acknowledge all known copyright holders of any photographic images used.

design by Jerlyn Jareunpoon

produced by Can of Worms Enterprises Ltd.

www.canofwormsenterprises.co.uk

Printed and bound in the UK by PublishPoint
from KnowledgePoint Limited, Reading

Contents

Someone walking down Crampton Street would not fail to see the contrast between the buildings on one side of the street with the other. Old and new. Long history and short. Which would they prefer?

The Story Begins!

Pullen's Estate is a very special place for me, and many others. I would like you to join me in celebrating this thriving community located in southeast London.

My twin brother and I were born in Lambeth Hospital in 1946 and then returned home to 138 Crampton Street. The interior was very basic – 1 bedroom, 1 front room where my parents slept on a "Put-u-up" bed, living room, kitchen and toilet. There was no bathroom, running hot water, or central heating! How did my mother, and others like her, cope? Mind you, we were considered posh because we had an inside toilet! On my marriage, in 1972, I left the estate. However, in 2006, I went to London with my dear friend David to show him where I grew up since he also enjoyed history. In response to his questions, I realised I knew practically nothing about the history of the Estate. So, my journey began.

182 Kennington Park Road

The Birth of the Estate

James Pullen & Son had a builder's yard on Amelia Street within the Estate and traded from premises at 73 Penton Place, which is off Kennington Park Road near the Estate. He acquired further property in the area in the 1880s, and following the demolition of some original houses, the first block of 16 flats was erected in 1886. Ever since the Estate was built, the family home was located just opposite Kennington Park at 182 Kennington Park Road.

On discovering that the land where the Estate was built had originally belonged to the Ecclesiastical Commissioners for England(5), I was granted permission to visit the library at Lambeth Palace. Whilst there, I looked through papers relating to the Pullen's Estate. It was such a daunting task, so I asked Stephen Humphrey, a historian from Southwark, if he could kindly read through all of the documents and piece together some relevant facts for the research. I have recorded these facts below and hope that they will be of interest to the reader.

The papers relate to the interest of the Ecclesiastical Commissioners for England in Pullen's Estate between 1879-1941. The Ecclesiastical Commissioners was founded in 1836 in order to take over historic endowments of the Church of England. In this case, they had taken over the historic land-holding in Walworth *of the Dean and Chapter of Canterbury Cathedral.* Subsequently, in 1948, the Ecclesiastical Commissioners became the Church Commissioners for England upon their merger with Queen Anne's Bounty. This was a fund set up in 1704 for the augmentation of the incomes of the poorer clergy. The bounty was the revenue from tax on the church prior to the Reformation and from the Crown itself after the Reformation (hence its name).

For many centuries, the Canterbury Chapter Estates in Walworth were run primarily as open land. The portions of the estates on the western side of Walworth were largely leased to the Penton family from the late 17th century to the late 18th century. By then, significant building development had begun along the Walworth Road. The predominant lessees subsequently were members of the Brandon family, descendants of Thomas and Samuel Brandon. The leases had been subleased, creating a complicated patchwork of tenure. But the Church, represented originally by the Dean and Chapter of Canterbury and then by the Ecclesiastical Commissioners, retained the freehold throughout.

The present documents relate to four plots, or parts of them, that the Ecclesiastical Commissioners labelled Nos. 17, 19, 20, and 32. The first and the last of these were only marginally involved in Pullen's Estate, but Nos. 19 and 20 were central to it. These two plots had been held under 99-year leases from Michaelmas 1786. The earliest of these papers, a letter dated December 3rd, 1879, states: "A Mr. Pullen recently bought the chief lease No. 20 with a view to negotiate for an extension of term for rebuilding". Apart from James Matthew Pullen's hopes as a developer, there was anxiety from the Church and its advisors that the existing estate had physically deteriorated, partly because the ownership of the subleases had been lost sight of. In short, some properties were without a guiding owner and were decaying.

A further letter of June 1st, 1881 refers to plot Nos. 19 and 20 "not disposed of to the School Board for London" (obviously for Crampton Street School) and to proposed leases for 80 years from Michaelmas 1885 at a net ground rent of £1,600 per year. James Pullen was to spend £50,000 on rebuilding over five years at a rate of no less than £5,000 per year. A succession of letters from Messrs dated between 1886 and 1893. Clutton, acting as land agents to the Ecclesiastical Commissioners, reported that James Pullen had built particular properties and that leases might be granted. The properties specified on December 15th, 1886 were on Iliffe Street and referred to an 80-year lease from Michaelmas in 1885 at a ground rent of £120 a year, the first rent to be paid at Christmas of 1886. The lease clearly took over from the 99-year lease of 1786. There are a few papers relating to the Duke of Clarence Public House, which was rebuilt around 1889 on the corner of Manor Place and Penton Place, a little south of where it had previously stood. A letter dated March 19th, 1941 states that Miss E.R. Pullen had become beneficially entitled to the whole of the estate's leases from the Ecclesiastical Commissioners on the death of her aunt, Mrs. E.L. Witcomb. Until 1941, the business of the papers still arose from the relationship of lessor and lessee between the Ecclesiastical Commissioners and the Pullen family.

The following is an excerpt from part of the Southwark Council's website:

> In November 1884 a Mr. J. Pullen applied to lay drains in Amelia Street and Worcester Road (subsequently renamed Iliffe Street) to serve a new development extending over the

entire block of land between these streets. These he numbered 2-23 Iliffe Yard, 1-96 Iliffe Street, 184-186A Crampton Street, 52-226 (even) Amelia Street and 25-56 Pullen's Estate, Penton Place. The group is remarkable in combining flatted dwellings with contiguous workshops in the mews behind. This combination of workers' housing and industrial units contrasts with the better known schemes by local authorities, Peabody Trust and Improved Industrial Dwellings Company which concentrated almost exclusively on providing housing alone. The closest comparison is with the series of tenements in Cannon Street Road and Rampart Street erected with roof top workshops by Jewish builders in 1893-5 recently identified by Andrew Saint. The Pullen's Estate is earlier and differs in having some form of workshop provision to the rear of every floor.

James Pullen applied for permission to lay drainage in 1884, before the first phase of the development commenced in 1886. From 1896 to 1898 James Pullen added another block to his estate when he developed land to the south of Iliffe Street in Peacock Yard. This is the only other section to survive. The estate was once much more extensive, running down a lot of Amelia Street and continuing to its south. The combination of flats and small workshops is still an appropriate one for the area, and forms the basis of a lively community. Original copies of meeting minutes, taken from discussions between the St. Mary's Vestry Committee (members who oversaw the parish, now referred to as councillors) and Mr. James Pullen, the builder, reveal that he had to obtain approval for each stage of the development i.e. drainage, roads, hoardings etc.

It was noted that in the 1898 Electoral Register, in St. Mary's Ward, Newington, a Mr. James Pullen was named as the landlord of 107 Newington Butts and 4 Clock Passage.

The Pullen's Estate was built by James Pullen & Son, the elder, a local builder who acquired the land and developed it from 1886-1901 (although he was planning the process in about 1884, and some say that the development went on a few years after he died in 1901). The Estate spanned across six streets, comprising 684 dwellings in 12 blocks. Attached to the rear of the dwellings, arranged around four yards, were 106 workshops. The names of these workshop yards were Clements, Iliffe, Peacock, and Clarence. Clarence Yard was pulled down when that part of the estate between Amelia Street and Manor Place was redeveloped to make way for the green open space and for flats which can be seen today.

The Pullen Family

James Pullen was born in 1823 in the St. Pancras district of North London and baptised on September 19th at St. George the Martyr Church in the County of Middlesex. There is no record of when he became a builder. According to the 1871 census, James, his wife Eliza, son James and daughter Eliza were all living at Douglas Terrace, Poplar, London, Middlesex (now part of East London)(7). In the 1881 census, his occupation is recorded as a lead burner, employing 2 men and 3 boys. His address was 73 Penton Place, Newington , Surrey (7). In the 1891 census, his occupation is recorded as being a builder and his address was still 73 Penton Place (7).

Sometime between 1850 and 1857, the family went out to Australia. This is known because on the 1881 British census it is mentioned that their daughter Eliza Lucy Pullen (who was aged 24 years at the time) was born in Melbourne, Australia which meant she was born in 1856-57(7). The family returned to England sometime afterwards. They may have gone out to Australia because of the Australian Gold Rush. If that was true, then James may have come home with a fortune! I obtained a copy of Eliza's birth certificate from Melbourne.

Holy Trinity Church, Marylebone Rd, London

Eliza was born on October 28th, 1856 at 202 Lonsdale Street East, in the district of Melbourne in the Colony of Victoria,

Australia and was registered on January 13th, 1857 in Melbourne, the parents being James Matthew and Eliza Pullen(9). James was recorded as being a plumber and was 34 years of age. His address was recorded as: London, Tipperary, Ireland, England. This was obviously a mistake because he was born around 1823 in Holborn, London (then in the country of Middlesex) according to census returns. The Registrar at the time must have been looking at the previous entry which also mentioned Tipperary, Ireland. Eliza Pullen (formerly Johnson) was aged 32 years and was recorded as being born in London, England. It was also recorded that they married in 1848.

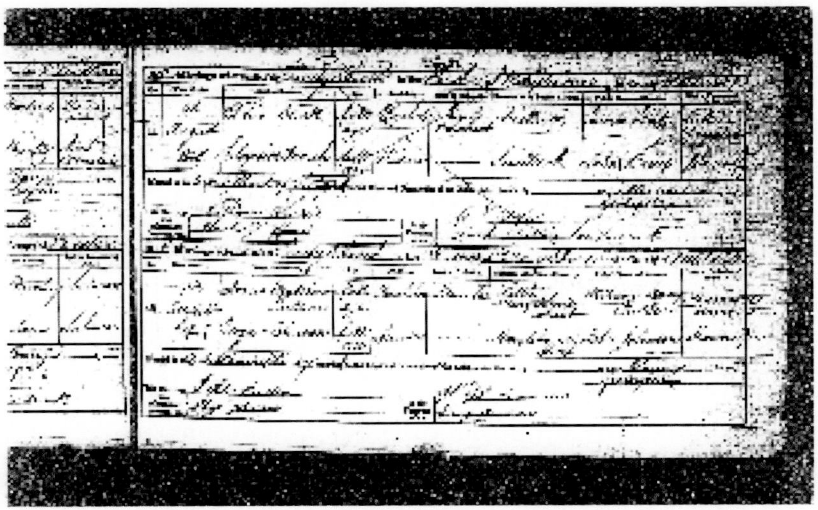

Marriage certificate of James Matthew Pullen and Eliza Johnson, 8th August 1848

I found the marriage detais of James Matthew Pullen to Eliza Johnson online. They married on August 8th, 1848 in Trinity Church in the parish of St. Marylebone in the county of Middlesex (3). James' occupation was given as a "plumber" and he was living on Little Marylebone Street whilst Eliza Johnson was living on Marylebone Street.

James' father, William Henry Pullen, had been a shoemaker but was deceased by this time. On the 1841 census, William's age was given as 40 as was his wife, Jane. Their son James (the builder) was aged 15(7). In that census, though, ages were either rounded up or down to the nearest five.
The address given at the time was Chapel Place, St. George Bloomsbury, Finsbury which at that time was in Middlesex(7). William died on October 9th, 1841 at Chapel Place in Bloomsbury at the age of 45 years. The informant's name on the death certificate was Sarah Buckland who lived at 9 Marchmont Place in Bloomsbury, London.

In the 1851 census, William was not recorded but his wife was aged 50 and appears in the St. John the Evangelist ward, Westminster as a laundress and is stated to have been born in Cockermouth in Cumberland(7). She was at that time living with her daughter Emily, aged 18, who was a housemaid and born in Lambeth, Surrey and her son Henry, aged 15, who was an errand boy and was born in St. Luke's Middlesex. This entry correctly excludes her husband who had died. James the builder, who had married by then, had moved away(7). James Matthew Pullen died on August 1st, 1901(3) at the age of 78 years. The cause of death was "senile decay of assimilative powers" and the address given on his death certificate was 182 Kennington Park Road.

His son, James Pullen, was the informant and present at his father's death. According to the electoral registers, James lived at this address from 1898 until he died. On the side of the wall, at No. 182 Kennington Park Road, there is a plaque with the following words inscribed on it:

FOUR AND HALF INCHES OUTSIDE THE FACE OF THIS WALL BELONGS TO J. PULLEN

I can only assume this relates to the little piece of land away from the wall. James Pullen's name still lives on today!

Below is James Matthew Pullen's obituary, printed on 10 August 1901 in the *South London Press*:

Death of Mr. J. M. Pullen.

AN INTERESTING CAREER.

THE FUNERAL.

It is with regret that we announce the death, which took place at his residence, 182, Kennington Park-road, of Mr. James Matthew Pullen, in his seventy-ninth year. The deceased was one of Newington's largest landlords, being the owner of model dwellings in Manor-place, Penton-place, Amelia-street, Iliffe-street, Peacock-street, Crampton-street, and Thrush-street, which accommodate in all 1,000 families.

Mr. Pullen had some interesting experiences in Australia. He was one of the young and stalwart members in that great army of adventurers which the magnificent gold discoveries in Victoria attracted in the early fifties, and after trying his luck on the fields of Ballarat and Bendigo, he took up the more certain and lucrative occupation of a contractor. At that period things were very crude, and one of the great difficulties was the water question, large areas of mining land having to be left because there was no water handy. Men had to carry "wash dirt" for miles to find water in order to abstract the gold, and in the majority of cases this was so difficult and expensive that they preferred to abandon their claims. At that time "dry blowing," the method of the alluvial miner in West Australia, was unknown. The conveyance of water from creeks in the neighbourhood to areas of "payable dirt" was very often carried out by crudely-built water-carts, but the high price of stock and the absence of roads made this a very unsatisfactory process.

It was therefore little short of a stroke of genius when one man, remembering the mill races of his native country, conceived the idea of constructing similar contrivances to convey the water from a creek to an alluvial area which otherwise would not have been workable at the time. The success which followed this enterprise at once made the idea of water-leads a popular one over the goldfields. At first parties of miners constructed their own leads, but the loss of time which this entailed and the delay in getting to work on their claims which it necessitated made the employment of other men imperative. By this means a number of men—Mr. Pullen being one of them—with experience in this direction found it more profitable to take contracts to do this work than to run the risk of ordinary gold-mining. Mr. Pullen was eminently successful, and was the means of conveying water in this way to the goldfields at Ovens, Castlemain, Wood End, and Pleasant Creek. As the goldfields increased and became more settled, more prominent works were required, and the connection which Mr. Pullen had already obtained amongst the early miners enabled him to keep himself constantly employed as a contractor in the many classes of work which the bush offered, such as railways, fencing, road making, bridge building, &c.

Having acquired a competence, Mr. Pullen returned to England in 1864. He took up his residence in South London, and commenced the erection in Newington of the model dwellings already referred to. He identified himself closely with politics, and became a prominent member of the West Newington Conservative Association and Club. Though repeatedly approached by the leaders of the party, he refused to allow himself to be nominated for the vestry or any of the other local bodies. Up till Christmas last Mr. Pullen was in the best of health, and that he was exceedingly popular with all classes was evidenced by the large number of floral tributes at the funeral. Some years ago the deceased commenced the erection, for his own use, of a handsome house adjoining his residence in Kennington Park-road, and though the house appeared from the exterior to be finished a couple of years ago, workmen had been engaged in the inside decoration up to within a few months of Mr. Pullen's death. Mr. Pullen leaves a widow and a son and daughter to mourn his loss.

The funeral took place at Brookwood Cemetery on Wednesday, the body having been previously conveyed to Woking. The three coaches contained: First coach—The widow, Mr. J. Pullen, Miss Pullen, Miss Nellie Pullen, and Mr. J. Witcomb; second coach—Mrs. Dent, Mrs. W. Hornby, Mr. Beckett, Mrs. Beckett, and Mr. H. C. Parker (Mr. Pullen's agent); third coach—Mr. Forge, Mrs. Forge, Mr. Clements, Mrs. Clements, and Mr. Huxtable (Mr. Pullen's foreman). Floral tributes were sent by Mrs. Pullen (widow), Mr. J. Pullen (son), Miss Pullen (daughter), Miss N. Pullen (granddaughter), Mr. and Mrs. Parker, Mr. and Mrs. Clements, Misses Clements, Mr. G. Davies, Mr. J. Witcomb, Mr. and Mrs. G. Witcomb, Mr. and Mrs. Tyler, Mr. and Mrs. P. J. Davis, Mr. and Mrs. Fordham, Mrs. Hutton, Mrs. Walters, Miss Wright, Mr. and Mrs. Forge, the employés, Messrs. Gadsby Bros., Mr. Hellchambers, Mr. and Mrs. Beckett and Mrs. Hornby, Mr. and Mrs. G. Ashdown, Mr. G. Smith, Mr. Newman, and Mr. Furby. At the graveside were Mr. G. B. Davies, Mr. G. Smith, Mr. C. J. Brown, Mr. Webb, Mr. G. Ashdown, Mr. and Mrs. G. Witcomb, Mr. and Mrs. Fordham, the employés, and numerous old friends of the deceased.

"Death of Mr. J. M. Pullen.

AN INTERESTING CAREER.

THE FUNERAL.

It is with regret that we announce the death, which took place at his residence, 182 Kennington Park-road, of Mr. James Matthew Pullen, in his seventy-ninth year. The deceased was one of Newington's largest landlords, being the owner of model dwellings in Manor-place, Penton-place, Amelia-street, Iliffe-street, Peacock-street, Crampton-street, and Thrush-street, which accommodate in all 1,000 families.

Mr. Pullen had some interesting experiences in Australia. He was one of the young and stalwart members in that great army of adventures which the magnificent gold discoveries in Victoria attracted in the early fifties, and after trying his luck on the fields of Ballarat and Bendigo, he took up the more certain and lucrative occupation of a contractor. At that period things were very crude, and one of the great difficulties was the water question, large areas of mining land having to be left because there was no water handy. Men had to carry "wash dirt" for miles to find water in order to abstract the gold, and in the majority of cases this was so difficult and expensive that they preferred to abandon their claims. At that time "dry blowing," the method of the alluvial miner in West Australia, was unknown. The conveyance of water from creeks in the neighbourhood to areas of "payable dirt" was very often carried out by crudely-built water-carts, but the high price of stock and the absence of roads made this a very unsatisfactory process.

It was therefore little short of a stroke of genius when one man, remembering the mill races of his native country, conceived the idea of constructing similar contrivances to convey the water from a creek to an alluvial area which otherwise would not have been workable at the time. The success which followed this enterprise at once made the idea of water-leads a popular one over the gold-fields. At first parties of miners constructed their own leads, but the loss of time which this entailed and the delay in getting to work on their claims which it necessitated made their employment of other men imperative. By this means a number of men—Mr. Pullen being one of them—with experience in this direction found it more profitable to take contracts to do this work than to run the risk of ordinary gold-mining.

Mr. Pullen was eminently successful, and was the means of conveying water in this way to the goldfields at Ovens, Castlemain, Wood End, and Pleasant Creek. As the goldfields increased and became more settled, more prominent works were required, and the connection which Mr. Pullen had already obtained amongst the early miners enabled him to keep himself constantly employed as a contractor in the many classes of work which the bush offered, such as railways, fencing, road making, bridge building, &c.

Having acquired a competence, Mr. Pullen returned to England in 1864. He took up his residence in South London, and commenced the erection in Newington of the model dwellings already referred to. He identified himself closely with politics, and became a prominent member of the West Newington Conservative Association and Club. Though repeatedly approached by the leaders of the party, he refused to allow himself to be nominated for the ventry or any of the other local bodies. Up till Christmas last Mr. Pullen was in the best of health, and that he was exceedingly popular with all classes was evidenced by the large number of floral tributes at the funeral. Some years ago the deceased commenced the erection, for his own use, of a handsome house adjoining his residence in Kennington Park-road, and though the house appeared from the exterior to be finished a couple years ago, workmen had been engaged in the inside decoration up to within a few months of Mr. Pullen's death. Mr. Pullen leaves a widow and a son and daughter to mourn his loss.

The funeral took place at Brookwood Cemetery on Wednesday, the body having been previously conveyed to

Woking. The three coaches contained: First coach—The widow, Mr. J. Pullen, Miss Pullen, Miss Nellie Pullen, and Mr. J. Witcomb; second coach—Mrs. Dent, Mrs. W. Hornby, Mr. Beckett, Mrs. Beckett, and Mr. II. C. Parker (Mr. Pullen's agent); third coach—Mr. Forge, Mrs. Forge, Mr. Clements, Mrs. Clements, and Mr. Huxtable (Mr. Pullen's forman). Floral tributes were sent by Mrs. Pullen (widow), Mr. J. Pullen (son), Miss Pullen (daughter), Miss N. Pullen (granddaughter), Mr. and Mrs. Parker, Mr. and Mrs. Clements, Misses Clements, Mr. G. Davies, Mr. J. Witcomb, Mr. and Mrs. G. Witcomb, Mr. and Mrs. Tyler, Mr. and Mrs. P. J. Davis, Mr. and Mrs. Fordham, Mrs. Hutton, Mrs. Walters, Miss Wright, Mr. and Mrs. Forge, the employés, Messrs. Gadsby Bros., Mr. Bellchambers, Mr. and Mrs. Beckett and Mrs. Hornby, Mr. and Mrs. G. Ashdown, Mr. G. Smith, Mr. Newman, and Mrs. Furby. At the graveside were Mr. G. B. Davies, Mr. G. Smith, Mr. C. J. Brown, Mr. Webb, Mr. G. Ashdown, Mr. and Mrs. G. Witcomb, Mr. and Mrs. Fordham, the employés, and numerous old friends of the deceased."

According to his will (2), the estate was valued at £105,474 3s 5d; quite a lot of money in those days! But in August 1902, the will was re-sworn because the estate was valued at £111,834 0s 0d. At the time he made his will on January 1st, 1898, he was living at 73 Penton Place (off Kennington Park Road).

James Matthew Pullen and his wife Eliza had a son of the same name born on January 26th, 1850(3) at 63 Broad Wall, which was near Blackfriars Bridge. On his birth certificate, it was recorded that the father James, the builder, was a plumber in 1850. The son became the works manager of James Pullen & Son.

He married Ellen Rosina Arnold on November 6th, 1883(3) in the parish church of St. Mary, Lambeth in the county of Surrey. James aged 33 years and Ellen aged 24 years. Accor-

St Mary's Church, Lambeth

ding to their marriage certificate, James was living in Penton Place, Newington and Ellen was living in Lambeth Road.

James' father was a plumber at the time and Ellen's father, Thomas, was an officer in the House of Lords.

In the 1891 census, James, Ellen, and their daughter, Ellen Rosina Pullen (the granddaughter of James Matthew Pullen, the builder) were living at 73 Kennington Park Road. At the time of his father's death, James was living at 15 Kennington Park Road(7).

James Jr. remarried on December 1st, 1902(3) and his second wife was Jane Henrietta Cullum, a widow aged 46 years. Jane died on April 4th 1939 at Elm Lodge, 50 Half Moon Lane, Herne Hill in the county of Surrey. In her will(2), she left £33,832 12s 11d gross. The net figure was £33,707 16s 0d. The estate duty was £3,715 3s 5d. Nothing else is known about James Jr., only what is mentioned above. However, according to the probate document relating to his will(2), he died on June 30th, 1909 at the age of 59 and was living at Melbourne House, Clarence Road, Clapham Park in the county of Surrey, which is now part of the London Borough of Wandsworth. The original gross value of his estate was £23,603 17s 11d and the net value of personal estate was £19,220 8s 0d. The Estate was then re-valued at £35,403 10s 8d dated August 3rd, 1909.

His previous address was 15 Kennington Park Road in Kennington, South London.

James Jr. inherited, and I quote from his father's will (2): "I give to my son James Pullen for his sole use and benefit the whole of my interest and lease in Couchmore Farm in Esher, Surrey with all the live and dead stock thereon."

The land on which the farm was situated is now a housing development and there are no surviving documents relating to the lease or to the Pullen family(6).

Ellen Rosina Pullen

Ellen was the granddaughter of James Matthew Pullen who built the Pullen's Housing Estate. She was born on 7th September 1884(3) and the address given was 76 Crampton

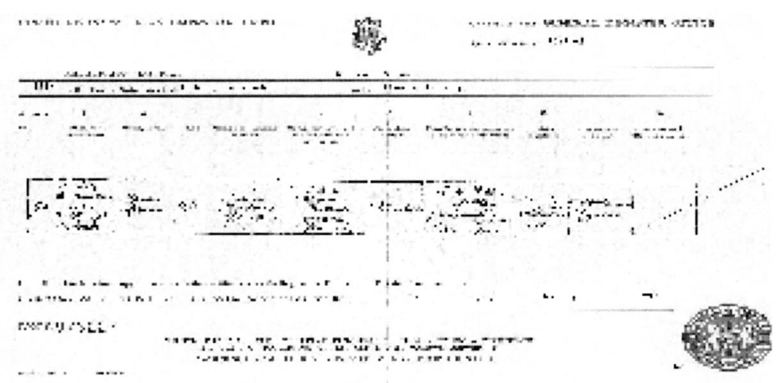

Birth certificate of Ellen Rosina Pullen 7th September, 1884

Street, Newington. This address was before the Crampton Street block of the Pullen's estate was built. Her parents' names were James Matthew and Ellenor Rosina Pullen.

According to my mother, every Monday morning, a chauffeur-driven car used to drive up to the estate's rent office in Amelia Street with two ladies sitting in the back of the car. The previous week's rent collections (less a sum of money which was held back by the rent office staff to be used towards any maintenance) were handed over and the car was driven off. I can remember taking the rent to the rent office on quite a few occasions before going off to school (this was in the late 1950s). One of these ladies could possibly have been Ellen Rosina Pullen, for she took a very active role in the Pullen's Estate and became the first director of Pullen's Estate Limited. This limited company came into existence on 11th November 1953, under the Companies Act of 1948. The other first directors were Joshua Henry Barham and Clifford Charles Lynn Randall. The nominal capital of the new company was £20,000 divided into 19,000 "A" shares of £1 each and 1,000 "B" shares of £1 each. I have a full copy of the document from Companies House which explains it all (4).

I don't know a lot about Ellen, only that she lived at the following addresses: 73 Kennington Park Road, Newington, London: "Knightsville", Clarence Road, Herne Bay, Kent; 30

Rollscourt Avenue, Herne Hill, SE London; 50 Half Moon Lane, Herne Hill, SE London and 116 College Road, Dulwich, SE London. According to the Land Registry, there are no records of her owning these properties(6). I knew that Half Moon Lane was part of the Dulwich College Estate, so I wrote to the College asking if they had any records of Ellen living at 50 Half Moon Lane. They wrote back with copies of documents dated 1934, in which the Estate's Governors granted permission for Ellen to construct an additional water closet at the rear of the garage belonging to the premises.

It would appear, from said documents, that the premises were on an 84 year lease from 25th December 1874 and that the lease was vested in Miss Ellen Rosina Pullen by 1934(8). I visited Half Moon Lane hoping to find No. 50 and to take a photo of the house, but Nos. 48-50 are now a small block of flats. The local postman happened to be delivering at the time and told me that the house at No. 50 was pulled down in 1988 to make way for these flats.

Ellen died on 2nd March 1957(3) at 35 Weymouth Street, Marylebone, London. I was able to find out that at that time, there were quite a few private nursing homes in Weymouth Street. Presumably, she died in one of those homes. On her death certificate, it mentioned that she was 72 years of age and was of independent means and was the daughter of James Pullen Jr. – master builder who was deceased at the time. It also mentioned that her official address was 35 Orchard Avenue, Shirley in Surrey. When I rang the local reference library and asked whether her name was on the electoral roll for that address, the staff checked back a few years and found it was not.

I can only guess that she lived there for a short period of time but I am not sure. The informant's name on the death certificate was A. Stokely, who was her nephew and was living at 116 Burbage Road, Herne Hill, London SE24. He was also a director of the company for many years and died in 2002. I found out after writing to the address that the occupier knew the nephew but had no knowledge that he was involved in the Pullen's Estate.

Ellen's will(2), which was dated December 1st, 1953 appointed Arthur Albert Stokely, who was her nephew, his wife, Marjorie Stokely, and Joshua Henry Barham, the Estate's manager, as her executors and trustees. According to probate, her estate was valued at £71,940 4s 5d. gross. After estate duty and other amounts were deducted, the net value was £69,608 14s. 6d.

The estate remained within the Pullen family until Miss Ellen Rosina Pullen, granddaughter of James Pullen Sr., died on March 2nd, 1957. Thereafter, the estate was run by directors of the former Pullen's Estate Limited company. The estate's officer at the time of Miss Pullen's death was Joshua Henry Barham, who had worked for Miss Pullen for over 40 years. In her will, she allowed him to live in the family home at 182 Kennington Park Road. Joshua had been a trustee and director of Pullen's Estate Limited before and after it became a limited company.

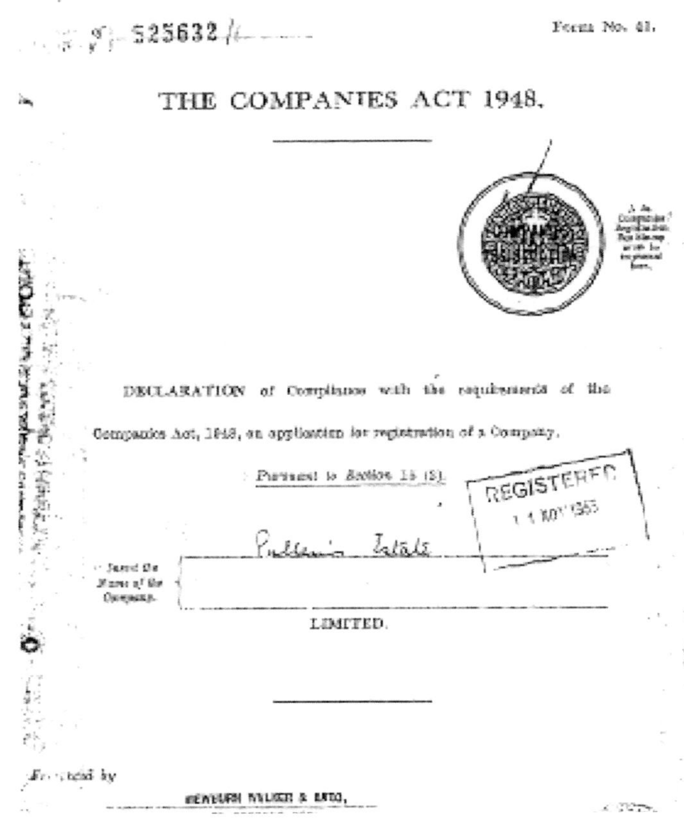
525632

Form No. 41.

THE COMPANIES ACT 1948.

DECLARATION of Compliance with the requirements of the Companies Act, 1948, on application for registration of a Company.

Pursuant to Section 15 (2).

REGISTERED

Pullen's Estate

LIMITED.

Presented by

Early History of the Estate

From the time the estate was built around the 1880s to when the limited company was dissolved in 2004, the Pullen's name spanned 118 years. Each time I have returned to the estate, it looks just as sturdy and well-built as it has always been. I continually feel very proud to have lived here for those 26 years. It is also remarkable that the name has lasted even to this day, and may it continue for many years to come.

In 1899, rents for 3 rooms, kitchen, and scullery were eight shillings plus six pence per week, which was charged for cleaning the stairs and gardens. Each incomer had to make a deposit of twenty-four shillings, which would in affect, bar any poor tenants. On a website by Charles Booth about the Walworth area, it mentions and I quote: " In Iliffe Street some *are* still building and old Mr Pullen in a top hat and fustian suit *was* on a scaffolding superintending; walls flush with the pavement but protected with iron railings from the street".

At the start of the Second World War, all of the railings were taken away. The reason given was that they were to be melted down for the war effort. Not so many years ago, my mother told me that the real reason was just to use the railings for scrap and to boost people's morale.

View of original buildings near the Manor Place end of Crampton Street, where part of the Pullen's Estate once stood. About late 1800s.

RENT BOOK

FOR

HOUSE AND PREMISES

situated

No. *66*

THRUSH STREET

NOTICE:—

Your Rent will be : *11* : *8* per week.

Increased Rates „ : *2* : *2* „

Total : *13* : *10* „

TENANT:—

M.

LANDLORDS:—

THE EXORS. OF

Mr. JAMES PULLEN

(Deceased),

65, PENTON PLACE, WALWORTH, S.E.17

When and Amount Due.					When and Amount Paid.				
1943		£	s.	d.	1943		£	s.	d.
Dec. 27			*13*	*10*	Dec. 27	[illegible]		*13*	*10*
1944 Jan. 3			*13*	*10*	1944 Jan. 3	[illegible]		*13*	*10*
„ 10			*13*	*10*	„ 10	[illegible]		*13*	*10*
„ 17			*13*	*10*	„ 17	[illegible]		*13*	*10*
„ 24			*13*	*10*	„ 24	[illegible]		*13*	*10*
„ 31			*13*	*10*	„ 31	[illegible]		*13*	*10*
Feb. 7			*13*	*10*	Feb. 7	[illegible]		*13*	*10*
„ 14			*13*	*10*	„ 14	[illegible]		*13*	*10*
„ 21			*13*	*10*	„ 21	[illegible]		*13*	*10*
„ 28			*13*	*10*	„ 28	[illegible]		*13*	*10*
Mar. 6			*13*	*10*	Mar. 6	[illegible]		*13*	*10*
„ 13			*13*	*10*	„ 13	[illegible]		*13*	*10*
„ 20			*13*	*10*	„ 20	[illegible]		*13*	*10*

Rent book from 1943

LANDLORDS:-

PULLEN'S ESTATE LTD.

ESTATE OFFICE, AMELIA STREET, S.E.17.

Agent:-

E. G. UTTON

RENT BOOK

FOR

HOUSE & PREMISES

situated

No. *66*

Thrush Street

TENANT:—

NOTICE

The minimum period for notice to quit by either landlord (or his agent) or tenant is now 4 weeks: Rent Act 1957, section 16.

When an Amount Due.					When and Amount Paid.				
1958		£	s.	d.	1958		£	s.	d.
Dec. 29			*12*		Dec. 29	[illegible]		*12*	
1959 Jan. 5			*12*		1959 Jan. 5	[illegible]		*12*	
„ 12			*12*		„ 12	[illegible]		*12*	
„ 19			*12*		„ 19	[illegible]		*12*	
„ 26			*12*		„ 26	[illegible]		*12*	
Feb. 2			*12*		Feb. 2	[illegible]		*12*	
„ 9			*12*		„ 9	[illegible]		*12*	
„ 16			*12*		„ 16	[illegible]		*12*	
„ 23			*12*		„ 23	[illegible]		*12*	
Mar. 2			*12*		Mar. 2	[illegible]		*12*	
„ 9			*12*	–	„ 9	[illegible]		*12*	
„ 16			*12*	–	„ 16	[illegible]		*12*	
„ 23			*12*	–	„ 23	[illegible]		*12*	

Rent book from 1959

Amelia Street, showing Air Raid Shelter

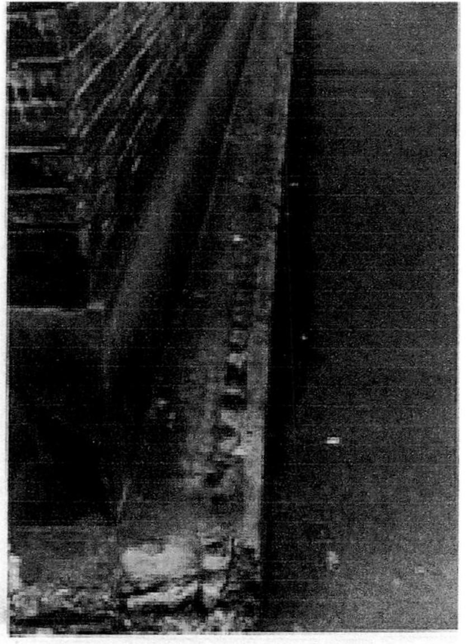

You can clearly see where the railings once were.

A typical front door to the block

The rent office in Amelia Street (white door)

Recent History

By 1967, it had become clear to both the directors and Southwark Borough Council that the estate was starting to fall into disrepair. Some tenants felt that the directors did not have the funds nor the inclination to do anything about improving the estate. In 1969, the directors wanted to retain the Estate, but Southwark Borough Council wished to purchase and refurbish it.

By 1977, several things had been decided. Firstly, the directors would have to sell the estate via a compulsory purchase order. The tenants, however, decided that they preferred to trust Southwark Council rather than a Housing Association to refurbish the estate. At the time, Southwark

Manor Place before demolition

Council was planning to do something major on the site and adjacent sites if they could get control of the land.

Finally, the Council obtained control of the estate and didn't offer any plans for its future, only to say that they intended to relocate the tenants elsewhere.

When it was made clear that the Council's intention was to demolish the whole Estate, several tenants and a Tory councillor took the Council to the High Court in London and won a reprieve for half of the estate. The Council then re-let to single people and couples because the Department of the Environment and the courts forced the Council to do so.

Looking down Penton Place from Manor Place before demolition of the blocks in the foreground of this picture.

It is interesting to note that as far back as 1973, the directors of Pullen's were negotiating with Southwark Borough Council regarding improvements to the estate, but these proposals were rejected by the Council. At that time, the directors understood that the Council was applying to the Minister of Housing for a compulsory purchase order covering the whole estate. If the application to purchase was granted, the directors were going to appeal against the decision, and that would take a considerable amount of time. Furthermore, in the Pullen's Estate Residents' Association newsletter dated December 1971, it is stated that discussions had taken place concerning modernisation and that in the Association's view, it was highly unlikely that the Council would take over the Estate-- either by agreement with the directors or by compulsory purchase. As we all know now, it was taken over by the Council, in agreement with the directors of the Estate.

In November 2006, I wrote to Southwark Borough Council (who purchased the estate from Pullen's Estate Limited in March 1977) to ask if they could provide me with copies of relevant documents, particularly relating to the sale of the Estate (all in compliance with the Freedom of Information Act 2000). After two months, they sent me all the documents. So on page 41, I have pieced together from those papers some of the history surrounding Southwark Borough Council's purchase of the estate(1).

The estate continued to be run by Pullen's Estate Limited until March 1977. The condition of the estate was deteriorating before this period and Southwark Borough Council was forced to step in and acquire the estate by means of a compulsory order. It may have been that the directors of the company did not have sufficient funds to carry out all of the repairs.

The Pullen's Estate Limited became an investment company after the sale of the estate went through in 1977. It remained as such until the company was dissolved on 11

December 2004(4). The directors of Pullen's Estate Limited invested the money acquired from the housing estate in various ways. I suppose when the company was dissolved, the investments were shared out between them. Also, as this was a private company, all of the relevant documents concerning the managing of the estate were held by the directors and trustees, not to be publicly viewed. The exception would be copies of the company's accounts, which I obtained from Companies House(4). I have recorded some information from one year's financial accounts on page 42 and top of page 43.

In the 1980s, the buildings between Manor Place and the southside of Amelia Street were demolished by the council, using their housing improvement powers. A park, plus housing, was developed on this area. The park is now known as Pullen's Gardens.

Some Architectural Facts

The estate is considered to be of special architectural and historic interest as a good example of a later Victorian speculative development that combines both tenement housing and workshop units with some shops. The residential buildings are four stories in height and each unit is three bays wide with an ornate central entrance to a common stairwell. The ranges vary from three to twelve units in length. They are faced with yellow stock brick, the front being enriched with the use of decorative terracotta arches to the door and window openings. The roofs are flat, providing amenity space for residents. The workshops attached to the rear of the residential blocks are simpler and more functional in appearance. They are two stories high and also built of stock brick and flat-roofed. The two-story loading bays are edged with blue brick quoins. The shops, flanking the entrances to the workshop yards, have traditional ly painted timber shop fronts with pilasters supporting a fascia and cornice and stall risers.

The estate, when built, consisted of tenement blocks on five sites over an area of 7.5 acres. Each block was of four-story construction with common stairwells giving access to two flats per storey. The original doors to the stairwells no longer exist. Each flat consisted of a living room, bedroom, parlour, scullery, and W.C. There are no bathrooms except where the scullery has been converted to accommodate a bath or shower.

Integral to the flats are two-story workshops. They were built to the rear of the flats and were like mews with cobbled yards. Originally, the ground floors of these buildings were designed to be stables with workshops above. All had direct entrances from the flats, which adjoined them even though many of the entrances were bricked in from the outset. Only a handful of the flats have an openable way through to the workshops now. There is a water supply to each workshop but no separate W.C. which is provided elsewhere.

The workshops have flat asphalted roofs, which are used as

gardens by the second floor tenants. This use was designed from the outset with wooden fencing separating each garden from the other. Ground floor flats have access to a small, enclosed yard. First and fourth floor flats can use the flat roofs of each block.

The Purchase of the Pullen's Estate by Southwark Borough Council from Pullen's Estate Limited (1)

Discussions took place in the 1970s regarding the above and on March 9th, 1977 an agreed document was signed by both parties as follows:

The purchase price of the property was £1,125,000 (which was £694,000 for the freehold and £431,000 for the lease-hold) paid by the London Borough of Southwark to Pullen's Estate Limited. This price also included all the workshops and the few general shops within the estate. It appears, looking through the accounts, that approximately £680,000 was paid to the trustees. This was because some years before they became directors and trustees, they could have been asked to financially help James Pullen by purchasing some of the land where Pullen's Estate was built upon. These three people could thus have had a vested interest in the whole project and quite possibly were paid that amount of money to be shared out between them.

Within the agreed purchase document, the rents for each tenant as of January 31st, 1977 are recorded. The copy, which I received from the council, had the tenants' names blackened out (which is within the terms of the Freedom of Information Act 2000). But for 140 Crampton Street, where my parents were living at that time, the rent was £2.25p per week!

The amount paid to the Pullen's Estate Limited was approximately £420,000, which was invested in shares and bonds until the company was dissolved on December 11th, 2004. It is interesting that when I obtained a copy of the Pullen's Estate Limited financial balance sheet for the financial year 1st April 1968-31st March 1969 from Companies House, the company had a number of shares invested in the following companies: Bowmaker Limited, British Glues and Chemicals Limited, Croda International Limited, British Engineering Limited, Allied Breweries Limited, British Leyland Motor Corporation Limited, The Cementation Company Limited, The Distillers Company Limited, The Dunlop Company Limited, The General Electric and English Electric

Companies Limited, Rank, Hovis, McDougall Limited, The Shell Transport and Trading Company Limited, and Smith & Nephew Associated Companies Limited(4). Quite a diverse set of company names back then!

One of the directors of the company was Arthur Albert Stokely, the nephew of Ellen Rosina Pullen. He died on the 4th September 2001(3) at 116 Burbage Road London SE24. The gross value of his estate, according to his will (2), was £763,663 and the net value was £756,914. His two sons, Peter John Stokely and Michael Charles Stokely, were also directors of the company and had been for many years.

Many of the present flats are local authority owned, but about 50% have transferred into private ownership. The price of these flats if one was buying now is about £250,000 – a far cry from when my parents paid just a couple of pounds rent each week in the 1970s! The purchase price for these flats now reflect the area as it is in central London, plus the fact that there are plans for a £1.5 billion development of the Elephant and Castle area.

PULLEN'S ESTATE LTD.

ESTATE OFFICE
AMELIA STREET
S.E.17

As you have already been informed by the Residents Association, negotiations have been taking place for the acquisition of the whole Estate by the Southwark Borough Council and I now have to inform you that these negotiations have been completed and that the Council will take over towards the end of this month.

You may recall that some years ago when a ballot was held amongst the tenants, a large majority favoured the Council acquiring the property as, in the economic conditions then prevailing, we were quite unable to find the money required to deal with the alterations and improvements suggested by the Council.

Therefore when the Council applied for a Compulsory Purchase Order we did not oppose it. The application was, however, turned down by the Minister at that time on technical grounds. However, we were informed that a new application for a Compulsory Purchase Order was being made and in order to save further costs and delay, the Council suggested that a sale should be negotiated by private treaty.

We regret very much that owing to economic conditions and inflation we have been forced to sell and thus sever all links with the Pullen family that have existed for nearly ninety years. We trust that under the ownership of the Council and with the continued help of the Residents Association, the same happy family community spirit will continue that we have always endeavoured to maintain.

A. A. STOKELY
Chairman

MARCH 1977

NOTE: Tenants entitled to a refund of the deposit paid may obtain a cheque for the amount due at the Estate Office after March 31st next.

The Yards and Their Occupants: Past and Present

Three yards on the estate, namely Clements, Iliffe, and Peacock are still in existence. It is not known precisely what trades were carried on in the very early days of the yards. However, at the time of the estate coming into the local authority's hands 90 years after being built, there were such diverse trades as industrial clog makers for the Fire Service, stationers, makers of ship fans, manufacturers of X-ray machinery, hat makers, brush makers, bookbinders, printers, furniture makers, and restorers. This included brothers J&J Lilleycrop trading as Turners Office Furniture. It is the only business still in the yards to have taken their workshop on whilst Messrs. Pullen were still the landlords.

Clements Yard, Iliffe Street, original frontage

Clements Yard, Iliffe Street, present day

Iliffe Yard, Crampton Street

Peacock Yard, Iliffe Street

The up-to-date list of trades within the three remaining yards (as of March 2013) are as follows: Architecture – Book publishing – Cashmere knitwear – Ceramics – Dress and costume design – Fashion – Film – Fine art – Florist– Furniture – Historic buildings repairs – Industrial design

– Jewellery – Knitting – Landscape design – Life drawings – Lighting design – Lute and guitar makers – Metal work– Painting – Portrait photography – Photography – Printing – Product design – Recycled bikes– Sculpture – Shoes –Silk scarves – Silversmithing – Soft furnishings – Theatre design – Textile design – Weaving – Yoga.

This original spirit of diversity of trades and occupations was resurrected in 1979 when several new businesses began to move in including silversmiths, fine artists, bookbinders, ceramicists, furniture designers, and makers; many of whom went on to achieve worldwide recognition, as well as operating as a vital part of the local economy. Many of these new businesses became involved with community projects such as school visits and demonstrations, college industrial experience placements, and indeed, some of the new businesses were started by graduates of local colleges – a trend which has continued.

The Pullen's Arts Businesses Association was originally formed in 1983 by Lutemaker, Stephen Barber and Fine Artist, Kevin O'Brien as a business tenants' association with the aim of representing tenants' rights and interests in dealing with the landlord, along with the Pullen's Tenants' and Residents' Association. The Businesses Association was instrumental in achieving the granting of an indefinite life for the remainder of the estate when it was threatened with demolition following its acquisition by the Council.

The following article was written by Jeb Loy Nichols in April 2006, concerning the smallest of the three yards on the Pullen's Estate, Clements Yard: "In 1988 I moved onto the Pullen's estate. As a full time artist and musician I was eager to rent one of the adjoining studios in either Iliffe or Peacock yards. When I approached Southwark Council I was told there were no vacancies. In the summer of 1989 I approached the Council about opening up and reclaiming the derelict site at Clements Yard.

The yard had been used as a dumping ground by permission of the Council to deter squatting. By 1989 the yard was ten foot deep in discarded household rubbish.

When I approached the Council I was told the site was unavailable and unsafe. I enlisted the help of a builder and we entered the premises and conducted a quick survey. There was no electricity or water. Most of the windows were broken, the stairs had collapsed and the ceiling was in need of urgent repair. But the walls and floors were sound and with some hard work it could be changed from a derelict site into working studios.

The builder and myself drew up some plans and a rough outline of what we wanted to do and we approached the Council again. This time they listened and said it was possible. Along with two other local artists we founded a co-op entitled "Fully Applied Arts" and drew up further plans and drawings of what we wanted to do.

In the autumn of 1989 we went to see Harriet Harman MP for Peckham and Camberwell and she was supportive and had several meetings with her staff and another meeting with the Council. In February 1990 we proposed that we, as Fully Applied Arts would take on the cleaning and renovation of Clements Yard in exchange for a rent-free period of five years. We presented detailed proposals for eight studio spaces and a small lunchtime-only canteen. This proposal was accepted and in the spring of 1990 the work began. We removed seven lorry loads of rubbish from the yard and four more from the studio spaces over the course of the summer. We also put in new walls, a new staircase, new ceilings and floors, new windows and a new toilet, as well as plumbed in water to each studio and full electrics throughout.

The renovation was fully funded by Fully Applied Arts and the work was carried out by its members. By the time work began Fully Applied Arts consisted of 12 members and by September 1990 most of the spaces were up and running. Clements Yard, once a derelict eyesore, was now the home of a glass worker, designers, wood workers, printmakers, jewellers and artists.

In the winter of 1991, Clements Yard opened and was an immediate success catering to the artists and craft people from the adjoining yards. The café remained open for a year until it was decided that the space should convert to badly needed extra studio space. In 1995 I left the yard to pursue other interests. During my involvement Clements Yard was (and continues to be) a thriving oasis of creativity".

Over the past 22 years, the association has been instrumental in achieving the working conditions, which have helped a unique creative community to thrive through negotiation and lobbying for such essential survival strategies as secure and tenant-friendly leases, as well as the more effective enactment of essential repairs and maintenance – and has in recent years essentially operated as a de facto management-partner with Southwark's Portfolio Management department. As the sense of community within the workshops has grown and developed, many unusual and/or highly specialised small businesses, leaders in their respective fields have come to the yards and in a few cases, sadly have gone. From Rob Dixson, the ceremonial sword maker/ to the Lord Mayor of London, to RimmingtonVian, the glassware and ceramics designer/decorator supplying various former royal palaces/stately homes and the National Gallery Collection, so many fascinating artists and craftspeople have called the yards home. Stephen Barber, the lutemaker from Peacock Yard, tells a story from the late 1980s concerning Mr. Fred Pace who was a veteran car fanatic and who garaged his 1930 Austin (bought new in

1935) in a ground floor workshop in the yard since acquiring it. Fred was born on the Pullen's and lived there all his life.

When Fred passed away, his workshop was cleared out by his relatives and friends, including Stephen, and amongst the Aladdin's cave of accumulated items (old car bits, tools, stacks of car magazines from the 1930s onwards being sifted through), there were two memorable items. One was an old bicycle, which had almost rusted completely away, and the second was a heavy cylindrical device.

Stephen's friend threw it to him and he was taken aback by its weight. When Stephen looked closer, he could determine it was about 10" in diameter and about 2 feet long with fins on one side and a Swastika painted on it!

Between Stephen and his friend, they decided they ought to telephone the police at Carter Street (just off Walworth Road) and let them know about it. The conversation went something like this:

"I've got a bomb," said Stephen over the telephone to the policeman on the other end.
"What?" came the reply.
"I've got a bomb."
"What are you calling me about it for then?"

"Well you probably know who we should contact."

A short while later, a police van arrived at the end of the yard. The police contingent pushed their youngest recruit forward who gingerly made his way down the yard towards Stephen who was holding up the bomb. Everyone else backed away. The policeman waved at Stephen indicating he should put the device on the floor. Upon the arrival of the bomb disposal unit, the yard was evacuated and the device was carefully packed in sand and taken away for detonation. It is understood that on detonation, the bomb blew a 50-foot-wide crater in the ground! This unexploded Second World War bomb must have been in Fred Pace's workshop for some 35 to 40 years!

The lady in the workshop, who wasn't in the yard on the eventful day, was none too pleased when she heard what had happened. What if the device had blown up in the yard during the interim period since the war whilst she was in her studio above? Just imagine the damage it could have caused. Meanwhile, the evacuation of the yard turned out not to have been quite as thorough as had been thought, because furniture maker, Allan Martens had remained in his workshop next door at No.1 throughout the scare, and no one had thought to check whether he was there!

Another amazing story was sent to me by David Kisler who used to live in England but now lives in New Zealand with his family. The following was emailed to me a few years ago: "Henry Kisler was my uncle (my father's older brother). He was born in 1902 in the Old Kent Road. His father also named Henry was a carpenter and set up his own carpentry business in partnership with his brother-in-law John Donaldson on 13th November 1905 and started renting in Peacock Yard. Initially they rented No. 8a but by 1908 it would seem they were also renting 2a. Their rent doubled according to the 1908 day book and there was a receipt for a sanding machine and electric motor. This motor sounded like the monster which ultimately drove all the machinery with wide leather belts and which I vividly recall on our visit to No. 2a in the 1950s. In 1910 A H Gadsby who operated from Nos. 1,2,and 3 Peacock Yard supplied all the shafting gears and belts to drive all the newly acquired machinery. Once set up I don't think anything was replaced or updated and in the 1970s the workshop resembled a working museum of early 20th century machinery. The firm grew rapidly and at the outbreak of World War One there were eight men, four apprentices and the two principals. After a year of war all that were left was one apprentice, one returned man and the partners. In 1916 two days after his 14th birthday, Henry Kisler (David's uncle) who I will call Harry as everybody else did to distinguish him from his father began work in the business. In 1917 John

Donaldson left the partnership to go to Handley Page making wooden aircraft.

Over time the Kislers occupied the following units:
1905 No. 8a
By 1917 Nos. 2a 5a 8a
By 1928 Nos. 2a 3a 8a
From 1948 to 1976 Nos. 1a 2a 3a

The Kislers called themselves fancy cabinet makers on their business cards. They specialised in what they called wooden inners or carcasses of cases for musical instruments, documents, jewels and regalia which were subsequently lined and covered with leather etc.

These were talked of as foundations for the leather trade. The family business also had connections with the Royal Family. It was through Harrods the famous store in Knightsbridge that the firm was asked to make cases for royal jewels and regalia for storage and travelling. I gather the process was that a royal tour would need a certain set of jewels and regalia and this would be measured and cases made by the Kislers and these would be lined and covered by others. Henry once reached under his bench and out of the pile of dust and shavings (he never believed in cleaning up and the floor was inches deep in debris) he pulled out a tiara which he had asked to be left for measuring and fitting but really just to show us children.

Queen Mary's dolls house in Windsor Castle

Another royal connection was with Queen Mary's dolls house in Windsor. The travelling trunks in the loft were made by the Kislers but as they were covered in leather you could not see any of Kisler's work. Henry joked that no one ever saw his work. Henry would start later and later during the day but would put in his 8 hours even into his 70s. Mind you a fair bit of the 8 hours involved talking. He had friends up and down the yard and his particular friends were Mr Hopkins a specialist printer across the yard and the man below who restored old cars. He also got to know one of the first of the new chums a luthier with whom he swapped scraps of rare wood. Henry Kisler his son, at the age of 25, took over as sole proprietor of the business in 1928 on the death of his father. Up until the 1929 depression about six men were employed. Henry finally had to lay off these men for lack of work and in a stroke of economic genius having guessed that commodity prices would never be lower bought up Polish plywood and American white pine his staple materials and covered the work benches of the now departed workers with wood completely filling No. 2 shop. Henry was still unearthing the benches when we visited in the 1950s.

One contract which I sensed kept the business afloat in the 1930s was the supply of Government Dispatch boxes (red boxes). Each government department had its own size and seemed to have an inexhaustible appetite for these essential items. I suspect Ministers on leaving office felt a few boxes a not unreasonable farewell gift! The Foreign Office had the largest boxes and the smallest went to the Palace. Queen Victoria hated the large boxes she was sent and designed a half size and lighter box for her use. The Budget box which you might recall the Chancellor of the Exchequer holds up outside No.11 Downing Street on Budget day was a Queen Victoria model and Harry felt it was probably made by his father. Other firms also made boxes but the Kislers kept making the smaller boxes into the 1920s. After the Second World War in which Harry joined the Royal Air Force he was back in Peacock Yard where the business picked up and in the 1950s and 1960s when we visited elaborate jewel boxesand brief cases seemed to be a staple. One-offs still kept Harry's love of trickery alive. Hidden compartments and secret drawers always amused him and in 1976 when he was about to retire and leave Peacock Yard he was asked to make a run of brief cases which were no more that a cover for a piece of armoured steel with a secret compartment to one side. These were to be held on the lap covering the chest when travelling through the more dangerous suburbs. Before Harry left Peacock Yard, Colin Sorensen, the Keeper of the new London Museum (a relative of my wife) came to look at the machinery and tools and took away a number of items. Typically Harry felt his stuff was of little account and sent Colin over the yard to a man who was still printing legal documents on a machine using quill pens! When the business finally closed in 1976 family and friends discovered fittings and tools and everybody got a few unfinished red boxes. Henry Kisler died in 1988. Whenever I visit London I take a trip to Peacock Yard. I cannot tell you what pleasure it gives me to find that others are now keeping the memory of that place alive".

Manor Place Baths

Characters: Past and Present

My mother and grandmother moved onto the estate in December 1939. They were allowed the tenancy because another member of the family also lived on the estate. I believe that when the Estate was built, only relatives of existing tenants were allowed within the estate. This does not happen now.

When I lived on Pullen's Estate, quite a number of families knew each other and it was a very friendly community. A number of police officers from the Whitehall and Lambeth divisions were tenants long before I lived here. The estate was known for being well maintained and I can remember my mother cleaning our part of the stairwell in our block each week. It was known in Walworth as "where the posh people live!" We had no bathrooms in the flats so we had to "wash down" in the scullery, which would be now known as the kitchen. We used to go along to Manor Place Baths for our weekly bath. As the taps were situated on the outside wall of each numbered cubicle, we used to shout out to the attendants when we needed more hot or cold water put in the large china baths.

On the corner of, what was then Hodson Street and Crampton Street and opposite the now FareShare shop, was the well-known green grocer, Harry Price and his wife. They ran the business for many years and people used to come from far and wide to buy their produce. I can remember quite often going along to the shop with a list of items from my mother. Harry would put a few extra apples and oranges into the bags without charging me.

Edith, who was born in 1911 and now lives near the estate, remembers the following: She was born in the Waterloo area of South London where her parents lived. Her mother died when she was quite young, so she went to live with her grandparents who had moved onto the estate in 1887 onto Amelia Street and had a balcony flat. She attended Crampton Street School on Iliffe Street in the original school building before it was bombed during the Second World War, and can remember that the building was very tall and had a Headmaster named Mr. Kenny for the boys and a Miss Benbow who was the Headmistress for the girls.

Edith knew Ellen Rosina Pullen, the granddaughter of James Pullen Sr., when she was a little girl and can remember Ellen as being "rather ladylike"! Edith mentioned that when Miss Pullen, as she was then known, walked around the estate and noticed dirty windows or curtains, she would report back to the estate's office and tell the staff to have words with those tenants to get the windows cleaned, or they would be out of the flats!

Rag and Bone Man

Edith also knew Mr. Barham and Mr. Hutton who were in

charge of the estate and rent office, and Freddie Holmes, who everybody knew because he was the maintenance man for the estate. Edith still remembers the ice cream horse and cart and the rag and bone man calling out "any old iron" with his horse and cart to collect anything that people did not want.

Ice Cream Man

Coal Man

Edith remembers the coalman delivering coal in sacks and having to go up the stairs into her flat and deposit the coal in a large container (which the estate's office provided) that was situated at the back of the flat. Edith also mentioned that in the early 1960s, there was a waiting list of about four years for people to move onto the estate.

Someone I met in Pullen's in 2010 said and I quote: "My experience of living on the Pullen's Estate has been a happy and positive one. It's very interesting to live in such a creative and vibrant community. The sense of community spirit among both long and short-term residents, whether they own their flats or rent, distinguishes the estate as a unique and special place to live".

Someone who works in one of the three yards mentioned (with no concrete evidence, only vague memories) that James Pullen used recycled bricks to save money, so this would date the bricks to about 70 years older than the estate. Because recycled bricks were used during building, when Southwark Council demolished half of the estate, they dismantled the bricks one by one and sold them to a third party.

A resident tells the story of how they came to live on the Pullen's :

"Sometime in the early 1990s I was visiting London from my home abroad and I happened to see Pullen's from the Wimbledon to Farringdon train. There was then no Oakmayne building to obstruct your view. I was fascinated by the cobbled yards and I thought how interesting they and the buildings looked – unusual and obviously just as they had been built – a Victorian rarity. I made a mental note to take a closer look when I could. Two or three years later a friend and I were in London again with a car this time and we came to take that closer look. I decided then that if I were to move back to London I'd want to live there on Pullen' Estate. It was close to central London, it was historic and it appeared to offer a type of community living which I wanted. Four years after that I was back and started to look for a flat on Pullen's. Through unexpected good fortune I got one almost right away because the person who had accepted it suddenly pulled out a couple of days before I came along. Life on Pullen's isn't always perfect and the buildings offer their own challenges (noise in particular). But I'm happy to be part of this exceptional community and to share with many fellow residents a commitment to the Pullen's community."

Another piece of history is that Charlie Chaplin, the famous silent movie star, claimed to have lived in one of the Pullen's flats in 1907. Also, supermodel Naomi Campbell lived on Iliffe Street. And of course, Roger Batchelor who lived on Crampton Street!

Louisa, the owner of The Electric Elephant Cafe on Crampton Street, records as follows:

"The good will and warmth towards me from Pullen's residents and artists in the yards meant that it didn't really matter that the cafewasn't ready when I opened it on that sunny day in September 2008. They were just looking forward to having the shop opened and used in a way that benefitted the whole community and to have new life breathed into the lovely building that is 186A Crampton Street. Being part of this community means the world to me and my business. It's an honour to be told on a daily basis that we are the hub of the community. I love introducing people to each other who will get on and many friendships and useful partnerships have been forged here. The Electric Elephant functions not only as a cafe and meeting place but also as a space for the yard's artists to display their work. So we are firmly rooted in the creative culture that seeps through the fabric of the buildings.

For me, one of the many great things about having a cafe here is the wide range of customers from all different back-grounds. People are fascinated by the history of the Pullen's Estate and it's really enjoyable to be able to share that with our customers. Quite a number of folk who used to live here have dropped by to tell us their memories of living on the Estate. People travel from far and wide to get a cup of "damn fine"; those lucky Pullen's people just have to roll out of bed!

Thank you to all those who have supported me.

The Electric Elephant is still a work in progress – so watch this space!"

Newsagent in Crampton Street. Now The Electric Elephant Cafe.

The Electric Elephant Cafe as it is today.

PULLENS
EVICTIONS
ARE
ILLEGAL

Campaign to Save the Remaining Flats

I was not involved in this long-running dispute having moved away from the estate in 1972, but I have pieced together various historical events given to me by some of those who were involved and also, by reading press reports. Others who were here at the time may have other recollections of events. It's a story of determination and a very committed community spirit between the tenants and squatters to save the remainder of the estate.

In 1977, families were re-housed elewhere and over a long period of time, some of the remaining flats were let to married couples, single people, and students who formed a tightly knit community and pressed the council to preserve the estate.

Squatters began moving onto the estate in about 1982 and eventually, the Pullen's Squatters' Organization (PSO) was formed to represent their interests, conduct negotiations with the Council, and to resist the planned evictions by the Council. The PSO believed that Pullen's was a special case within Southwark because of its age and the workshops attached to the estate.

In 1985, before the decision was made to give the estate life-long status, the Council was scarcely letting any properties. During this period, there were flats that had legitimate tenants occupying them. The Tenants' Association revealed that there were about 48 empty flats which were occupied by squatters with the full support of the Tenants' Association.

Many of these properties were in an appalling state of repair and the squatters had devoted large amounts of skill, time and money to improving their homes and saving them from dereliction.

During the long drawn out legal procedures regarding evictions by the Council, there began an interest from MPs and the local press. Also, the Tenants' Association supported the

PSO and were determined that the council would not evict anybody. Both the TA and the PSO were fighting for their future within the Estate.

As the temperature increased, more politicians became involved – some sympathetic – but of course unable to help. The squatters were eventually told "off the record" that the Council might be willing to consider offering tenancies to those squatters who were on the waiting list, but not necessarily on the estate and definitely not in the flats they were squatting. This was rejected by the squatters, as many of them had taken on flats and renovated them (sometimes very nicely) and so the squatters waited for the evictions. According to eye witnesses, this was the event which took place in 1985 concerning the attempted evictions. The police turned up in force with removal lorries and an army of bailiffs. They closed all the local roads and deployed the riot squad on the Pullen's open space, which then was a patch of waste ground. The squatters were warned of the pending operation by an air raid siren going off, which was situated on a roof on Amelia Street. This was removed when the Council did repairs to the parapet wall. A point of interest has always been to find out how an anonymous protestor painted the word "SHAME" in 50-foot-high letters across the front of the Thrush Street block, prior to the demolition of that part of the estate! The perpetrator has never been identified.

A number of flats were barricaded by squatters, with television crews from Europe filming the operation. Residents from nearby Hughes House (the sheltered unit) confronted the riot police. Pensioners started waving their fingers in the faces of a double row of police in boiler suits and full-length shields. The evictions were not very successful and it took all day to secure 16 evictions.

This was largely due to the architecture, which meant a barricade could be built on the inside of the front door to a parallel wall 18 inches thick and about three feet away. The bailiffs had to take out the doors forward because it was impossible to break them in. The bailiffs and police failed to recognise that you could move from one stairwell to another over the roofs and along the balconies at the back. This allowed for a sustained bombardment from the roofs, with the help of appropriate materials saved and stored for the purpose over a number of weeks.

The device of painting out the flat numbers at the entrance to the stairwells also caused considerable confusion. The police and bailiffs were met by a musical band, probably playing something along the lines of "We Shall Not Be Moved!"

Despite the high emotions, there were only three arrests and subsequently all charges were dropped, with the exception of damage to a policeman's uniform and costs of about £50 were ordered to replace it. It had been hit by ink squirted from a letterbox by the incumbent squatter.

The squatters had barricaded themselves in their flats and some had poured cooking oil on the landings outside their doors to make it difficult for the bailiffs to smash their doors down. The first people to be served notice lived in Penton Place, so they changed their door locks and because of this, the whole eviction process had to start all over again! The evictions were eventually carried out, and of course those who had been evicted immediately broke back into their flats. Negotiations with the Council followed, which resulted in squatters on the housing list being granted tenancies but still not in the flats they squatted. However, the Council would expedite mutual transfers, so if you had been granted your friend's flat you could exchange and stay where you were. Some of course accepted nicer flats than the ones they were in! A somewhat comical period followed, in which people moved round the corner or a few doors away.

Some of the squatters who were painters, carpenters, plumbers etc. decided to smarten up their flats, and some went on to earn a living putting in hot water systems and bathrooms as tenants were eligible for home improvement grants.

So, the moral of this incredible story is that a plumber (James Pullen started out as a plumber before becoming a master builder) built the estate and it could be argued that plumbers saved it!

The demolition of the rest of the estate was prevented when squatters, intent on preserving the remainder of an individual late Victorian estate, occupied some of the blocks. The original number of flats stood at 684 and comprised a total of 85 blocks. After partial demolition, the total number of flats now stands at 352 and 44 blocks. The flats are as follows: 56 in Penton Place, 88 in Amelia Street, 96 in Iliffe Street, 48 in Peacock Street, and 64 in Crampton Street. The total number of steps in all the blocks are 2,464 if you want to climb each one! I must say at this point that Pullen's Estate is now only one of a few surviving Victorian estates left in London – and I was a part of its history!

others an open day event in the studio. I spoke about the research and Alan spoke about the workshops. Stephen Humphrey showed various slides about the whole area and Southwark in general. That event certainly generated quite an amount of interest in the research. Thanks Alan for your support and interest.

To the staff of the Peckham branch of the Southwark Resource Centre for helping to design the posters and printing and laminating them. This also includes Angela Lucas, the PTA treasurer at the time, who has given me advice on the posters. Many thanks to the Pullen's Tenants' Association Committee for allowing me to have the Pullen's Centre for various occasions.

OYSTER COURT

COOPERATIVE FUNERALS
COUPONS TAKEN
COME AND MEET HIM

YOU
TO RESIST
'FLU

The King's Speech: Pullen's International Film Fame

(if only for a few minutes and two clips)!

At the end of 2009, a film crew descended onto the estate for a few days, shooting for "The King's Speech", which tells the story of the present Queen's father, George VI's speech impediment.

The reason why the film shooting was done on the Estate was because the flats resembled the ones in North London where George VI went for his speech therapy. Those buildings no longer exist. Louisa kindly emailed me a photo gallery, showing various clips of the filming, so below are a few of them. The film went on general release in the U.K. in January of 2011 and has been a tremendous success having won 7 BAFTA awards and 4 awards at the OSCARS.

NOURISHES
YOU
TO RESIST
'FLU

FASCISM IS PRACTICAL
FASCISM IS PRACTICAL
STAND BY THE KING
STAND BY THE KING
STAND BY THE KING
STAND BY THE KING
STAND BY THE KING
GOD SAVE THE KING
GOD SAVE OUR KING
GOD SAVE OUR KING
GOD SAVE OUR KING
GOD SAVE OUR KING
GOD SAVE THE KING
GOD SAVE THE KING

A Few Further Notes on James Pullen

Reproduced from the *Southwark Remembrancer* by permission of Stephen Humphrey

In the life of James Matthew Pullen, several facts have been established by research. The central one is that he was trained as a plumber and that he remained in that trade ever after. A surprising one is that he went to Australia, where his daughter was born at Melbourne in Victoria. He is shown to have come back from there long before he started to build Pullen's Estate in Walworth. Perhaps the most surprising fact is that he did not begin to do so until he was in his sixties. And at his death in 1901, he was clearly very rich. How can we explain his career?

He seems to have had a close friendship with the editor of the South London Chronicle, who had obviously heard many stories from him. We forget how small the world of a local editor or of a local politician would have been in the later 19th century. A vestry or council ruled over a rather tiny borough; the Vestry of St. Mary Newington covered little more than Walworth. Unfortunately for us, Pullen never became an elected politician, and so we lack the constant reporting of his speeches which we would otherwise have had, not to mention photographs of him. But he eventually became a public figure and above all a rich one.

Like many Englishmen in the mid-19th century, he clearly went to

Australia to make his fortune in the goldfields. He failed in that quest, but he did attainwhat was termed 'a competence' through his plumber's knowledge in supplying the workings with water, and then by using his expertise to connect houses in Melbourne to water mains. Back in England, he was definitely not rich, as we can see from the very small number of men he employed at the time of the census in 1871. He seems to have tried his hand in the U.S.A., too, but for just a brief period, and almost certainly before 1871. What made his fortune then followed.

It was a plumbing invention, apparently a drain-tap. More research is now needed to find the patent or patents that were involved, but his entries in directories provide good clues to timing. [We already know from tile-deeds and from correspondence with the Ecclesiastical Commissioners, the local freeholders, that he was looking at a building project as early as 1879. The 1870s were therefore crucial.] So an invention was his first fruitful 'goldfield', which gave him money for his tenement blocks. But there was one further source of income: the need for workshop space is alleged to be the original reason for the workshops arranged in yards. I can see that this might have explained the first set of workshops, but it seems unlikely that it underlay the later ones; by then, it must have become a habit, perhaps because it paid well. Research is now needed in the rate books on the occupiers of the yards in the early days of the Estate, and additionally, in newspapers in the 1870s and 1880s. But I do think that the basic problems of explaining his career now have plausible answers.

Stephen Humphrey.

Conclusion

When I first decided to research the Pullen's Estate in 2006, it was for my interest, only having lived there for 26 years with my parents. For myself and my parents, and I expect for many other tenants, it was a home. My parents knew that the estate was a private concern, owned and managed by the Pullen's Estate Limited, and that is all they knew. During my research, I decided to produce a book so that as many people who live and work within the Pullen's community could have the opportunity to learn a little bit of its history.

Over these past few years, I have met many residents, tenants and those who work in the three remaining yards within the workshops. They have all made my visits enjoyable and also, have expressed an interest in the research. There have been many occasions when I have travelled up from my home town of Crawley– not to do the research but to meet up with friends I have got to know quite well, and the Electric Elephant Café has always been the focal meeting place. This has enabled me to build up a relationship with these people, which has enriched my research and I will always be grateful for their friendship, support and advice.

I personally think that this is a fascinating story of one man's vision of building a vast estate to include originally four yards which comprised so many small workshops. In the early days, those who were living on the ground floor would have had direct access straight into their workshops.

The Pullen's name has spanned over 134 years from about 1879 when the estate was first planned, up to the present day. Although the family and the limited company which was dissolved in 2004 are no longer involved, the name lives on and hopefully, it will for many years to come – maybe for another 100 years! A masterpiece of the Victorian era!

Ironically, the one photo I have not been able to find after extensive searching is that of the great man himself – MR. JAMES PULLEN. If anyone has a photo or knows where I can obtain one, I would be extremely grateful. Just pop in to The Electric Elephant Cafe and Louisa will pass it on to me.

Finally, I very much hope that you have enjoyed reading the Pullen's history as much as I have in researching it and that it will be passed on to future generations!

I was born in 1946 in Lambeth Hospital, which was then situated in Brooke Drive, near the Elephant and Castle. My home was on the Pullen's Estate in Crampton Street. My mother and grandmother first moved on to the Estate in December 1939. I lived there until 1972 when I married my wife Jackie. We initially lived at Crystal Palace, then West Norwood and finally, in 1979, we moved to Crawley in West Sussex.

REFERENCES

1 Southwark Borough Council

2 Wills and Probate Office, London

3 General Registry Office for England and Wales

4 Companies House

5 Lambeth Palace Library

6 Land Registry Office

7 Office of National Statistics

8 Dulwich College Estate Office

9 Australian Census (Melbourne, Victoria)

For additional copies of *The Pullen's Story | 1879 – Present Day* please visit: www.canofwormsenterprises.co.uk

Also available on the history of the Pullen's Yards is:
Made in Southwark: A Photographic Celebration of the Hand
featuring photographs by George Nicholson of former artisans and occupants of the Yards.